John Thompson's Modern Course for the Piano — Second Grade

CHRISTMAS PIANO SOLOS

ISBN 978-1-4234-5690-2

WILLIS MUSIC

Exclusively Distributed By

HAL•LEONARD®

7777 W. Bluemound Rd. P.O. Box 13819 Milwaukee, WI 53213

Visit Hal Leonard Online at
www.halleonard.com

Contents

Frosty the Snow Man

Use with John Thompson's Modern Course for the Piano
SECOND GRADE BOOK, after page 6.

Words and Music by Steve Nelson
and Jack Rollins
Arranged by Glenda Austin

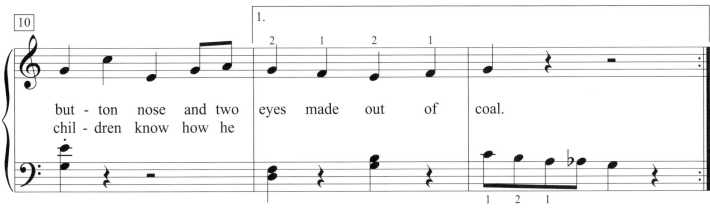

4

came to life one day. There must have been some mag - ic in that

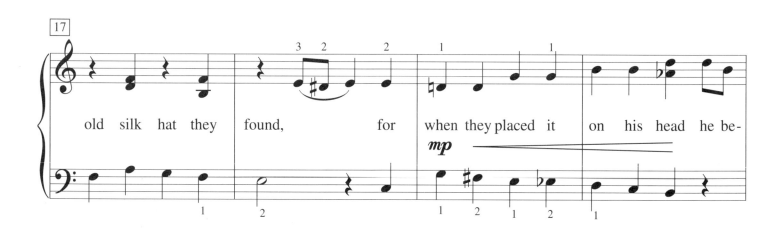

old silk hat they found, for when they placed it on his head he be-

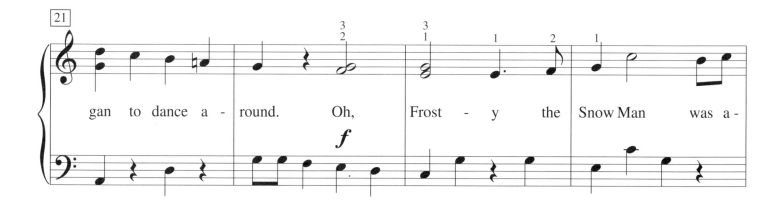

gan to dance a - round. Oh, Frost - y the Snow Man was a-

live as he could be, and the chil - dren say he could laugh and play just the

same as you and me. Thump-et - y thump thump, thump-et - y thump thump,

mf

look at Frost - y go. Thump - et - y thump thump,

thump - et - y thump thump, o - ver the hills of snow.

mp

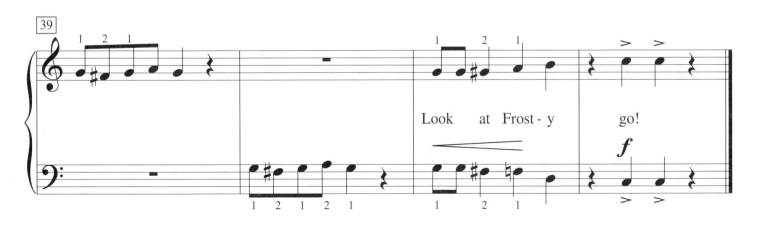

Look at Frost - y go!

f

Dance of the Sugar Plum Fairy

from THE NUTCRACKER

Use after page 11.

By Pyotr Il'yich Tchaikovsky
Arranged by Glenda Austin

Delicately

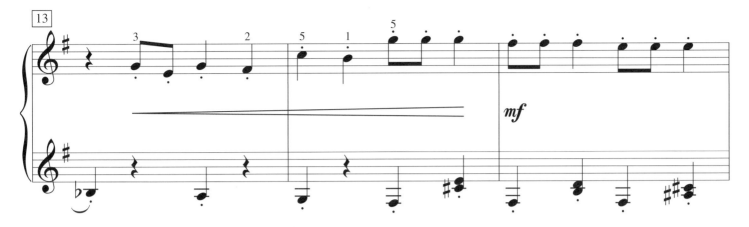

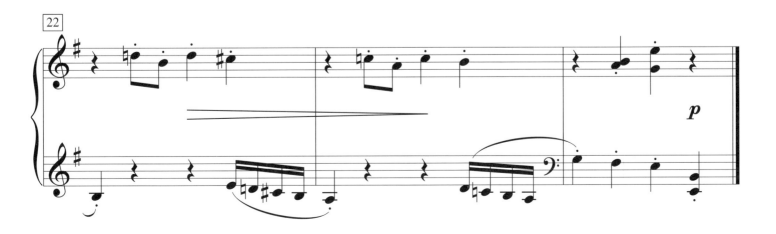

I Heard the Bells on Christmas Day

Use after page 18.

Words by Henry Wadsworth Longfellow
Adapted by Johnny Marks
Music by Johnny Marks
Arranged by Glenda Austin

Not too fast

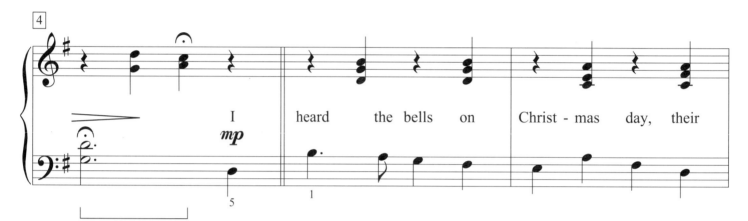

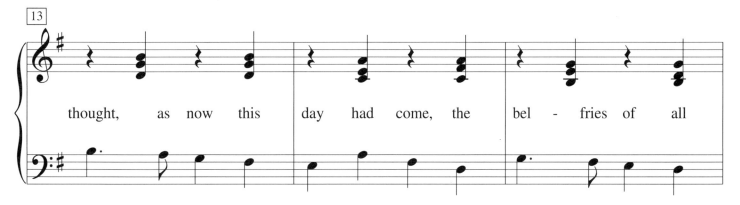

thought,   as   now   this   day   had   come,   the   bel - fries   of   all

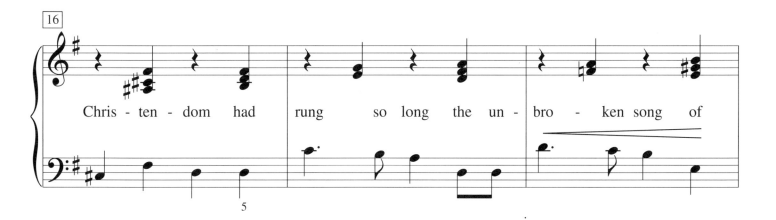

Chris - ten - dom   had   rung   so   long   the   un - bro - ken song   of

peace   on   earth,   good   will   to   men.

poco rit.

mf

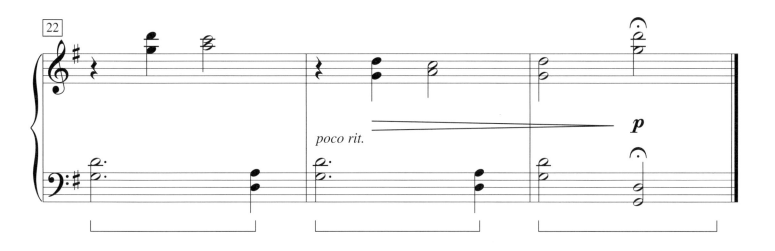

poco rit.

p

I Saw Mommy Kissing Santa Claus

Use after page 23.

Words and Music by Tommie Connor
Arranged by Glenda Austin

With excitement!

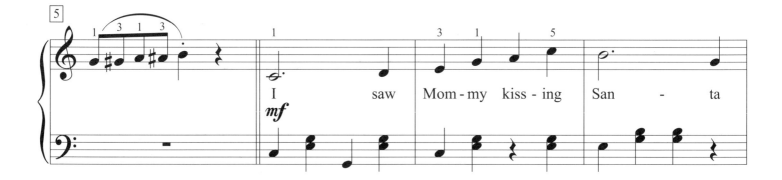

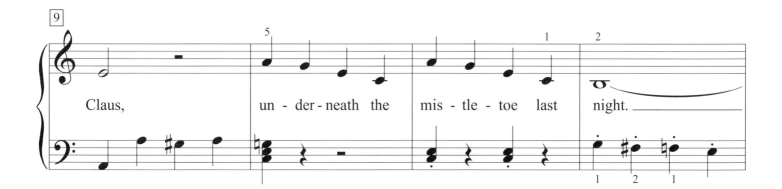

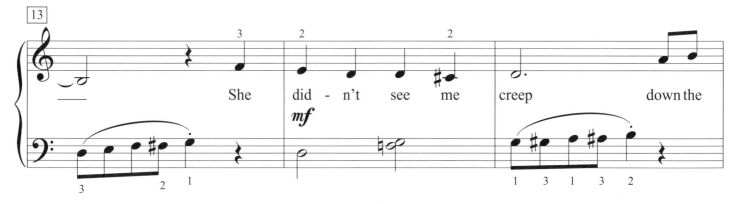

stairs to have a peep, she thought that I was tucked up in my

bed-room fast a-sleep. Then I saw Mom-my tick-le

San - ta Claus, un-der-neath his beard so snow-y

white. _____ Oh, what a laugh that would have

been, if Dad - dy had on - ly seen Mom - my

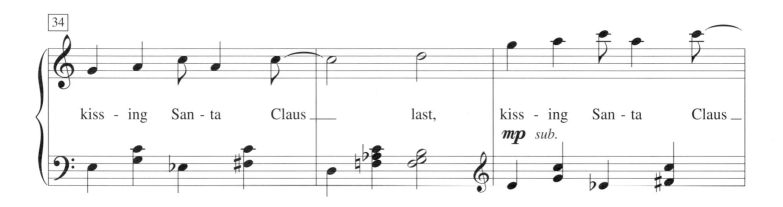

kiss - ing San - ta Claus ___ last, kiss - ing San - ta Claus ___

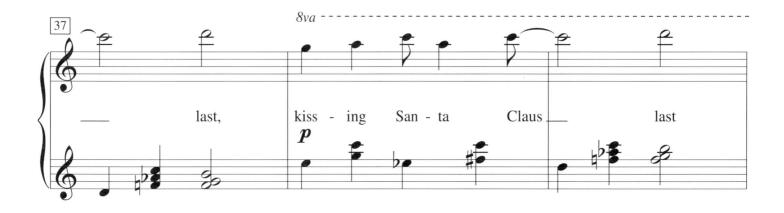

___ last, kiss - ing San - ta Claus ___ last

night.

The Chipmunk Song

Use after page 28.

Words and Music by Ross Bagdasarian
Arranged by Glenda Austin

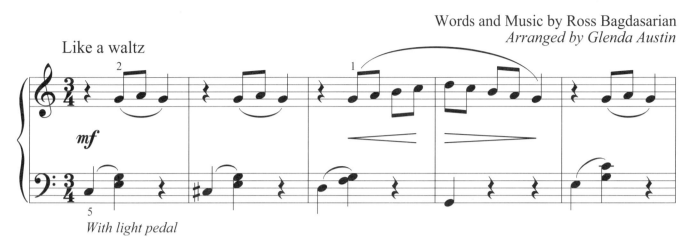

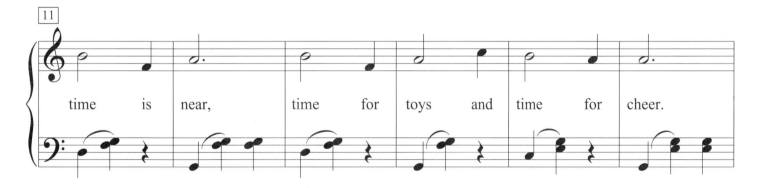

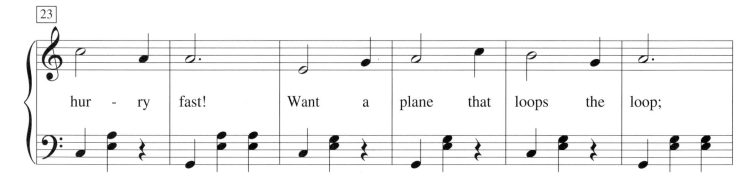

hur - ry fast! Want a plane that loops the loop;

me, I want a hu - la hoop. We can hard - ly

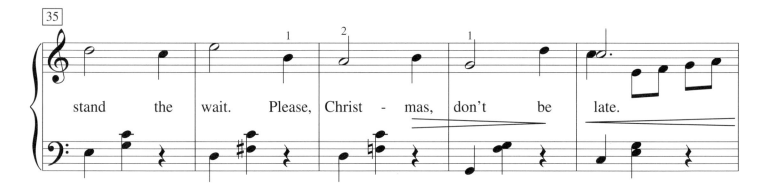

stand the wait. Please, Christ - mas, don't be late.

mf cantabile

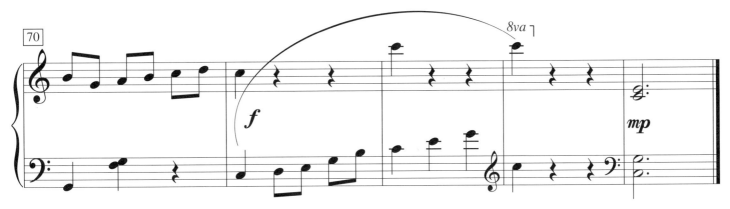

My Favorite Things

from THE SOUND OF MUSIC

Use after page 33.

Lyrics by Oscar Hammerstein II
Music by Richard Rodgers
Arranged by Glenda Austin

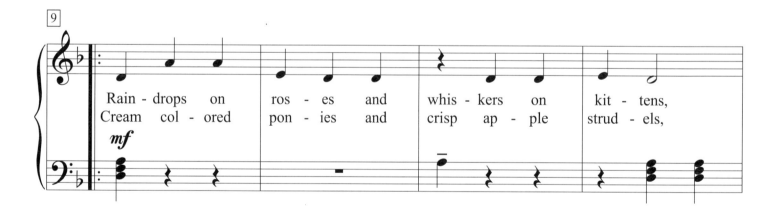

Rain - drops on ros - es and whis - kers on kit - tens,
Cream col - ored pon - ies and crisp ap - ple strud - els,

Bright cop - per ket - tles and warm wool - en mit - tens,
Door - bells and sleigh bells and schnit - zel with noo - dles,

Brown pa - per   pack - a - ges   tied up with   strings,   These are a
Wild geese that   fly with the   moon on their   wings,

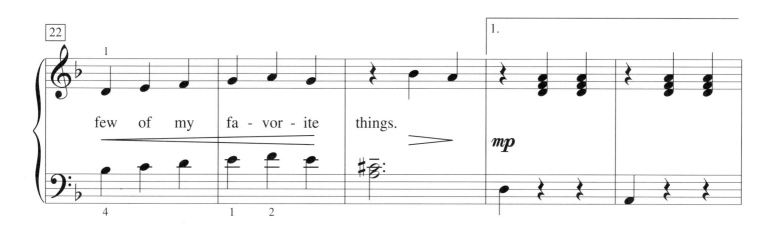

few of my   fa - vor - ite   things.   *mp*

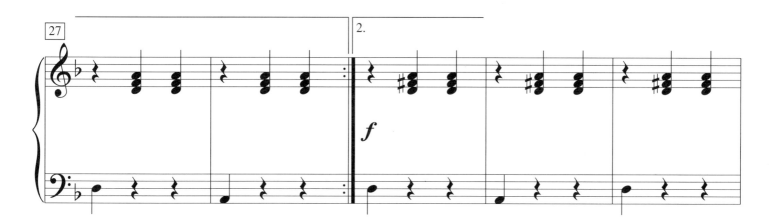

f

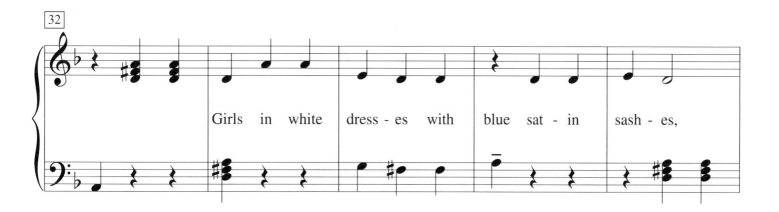

Girls in white   dress - es with   blue sat - in   sash - es,

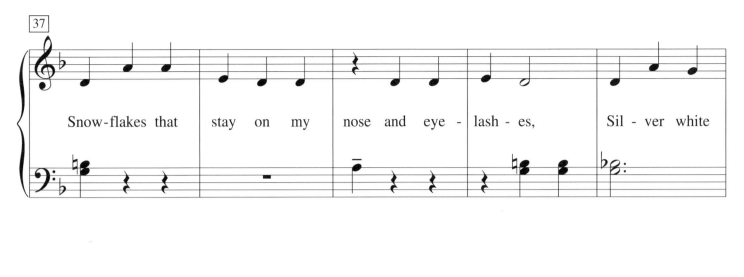

Snow-flakes that stay on my nose and eye - lash - es, Sil - ver white

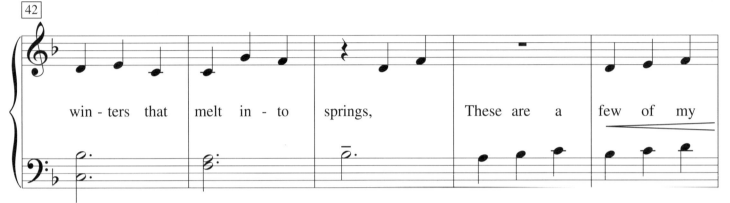

win - ters that melt in - to springs, These are a few of my

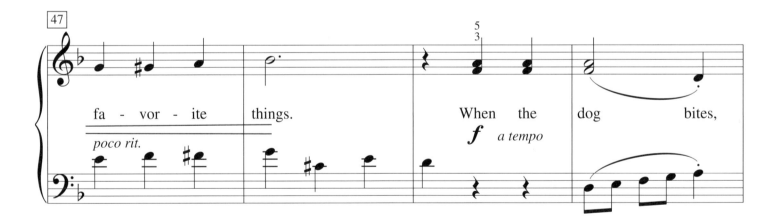

fa - vor - ite things. When the dog bites,

poco rit. **f** *a tempo*

when the bee stings, When I'm feel - ing

sad, I sim - ply re - mem - ber my

fa - vor - ite things ____ and then I don't feel

broaden so bad. a tempo

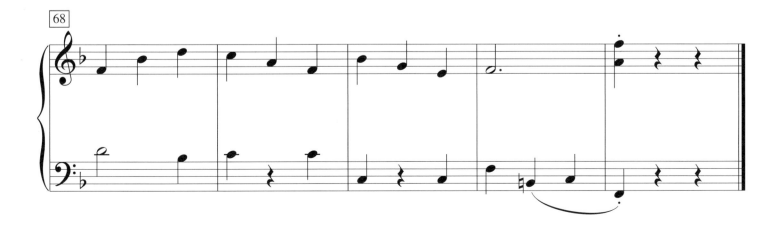

Let It Snow! Let It Snow! Let It Snow!

Use after page 39.

Words by Sammy Cahn
Music by Jule Styne
Arranged by Glenda Austin

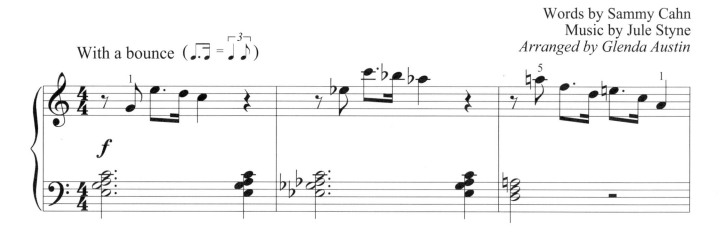

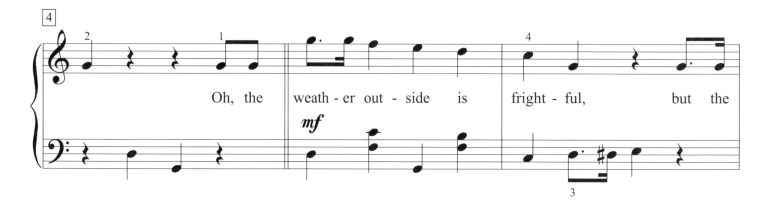

Oh, the weath-er out-side is fright-ful, but the

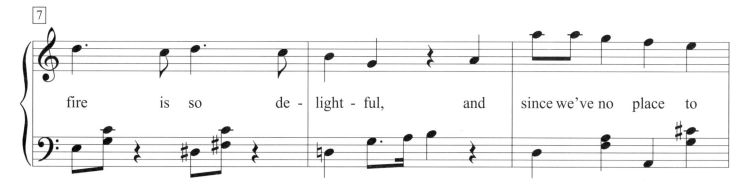

fire is so de-light-ful, and since we've no place to

go, Let it snow! Let it snow! Let it snow! It

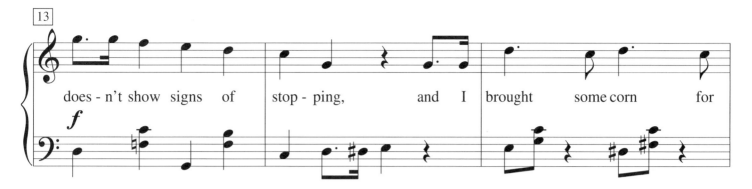

does - n't show signs of stop - ping, and I brought some corn for

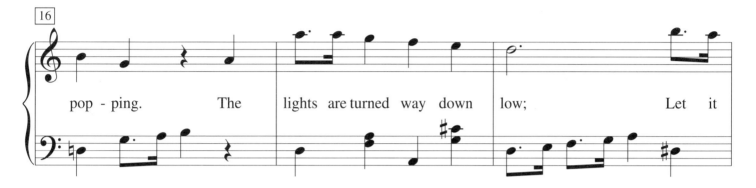

pop - ping. The lights are turned way down low; Let it

snow! Let it snow! Let it snow! When we fi - nal - ly kiss good -

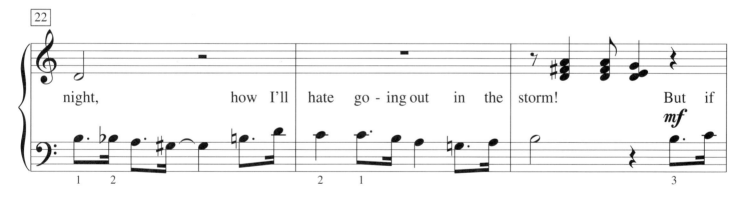

night, how I'll hate go - ing out in the storm! But if

you'll real - ly hold me tight, all the way home I'll be

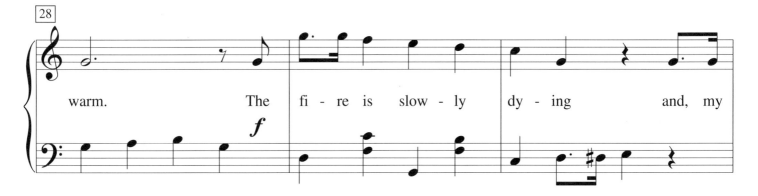

warm.　　The　fi - re　is　slow - ly　dy - ing　　and, my

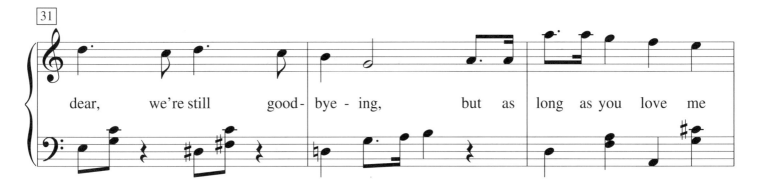

dear,　we're still　good- bye - ing,　but　as　long　as you　love　me

so,　　Let　it　snow! Let　it snow! Let　it　snow!

Jingle, Jingle, Jingle

Use after page 51.

Music and Lyrics by Johnny Marks
Arranged by Glenda Austin

Sparkling

mf *playfully*

Jin - gle, jin - gle, jin - gle, you will hear my sleigh bells ring,

detached (both hands)

I am old Kris Krin - gle, I'm the king of jin - gl - ing.

Jin - gle, jin - gle rein - deer, through the frost - y air they'll go,

they are not just plain deer, they're the fast-est deer I know. (Ho! Ho!) You

must be-lieve that on Christ-mas Eve I won't pass you by. I'll

dash a-way in my mag-ic sleigh, fly-ing through the sky.

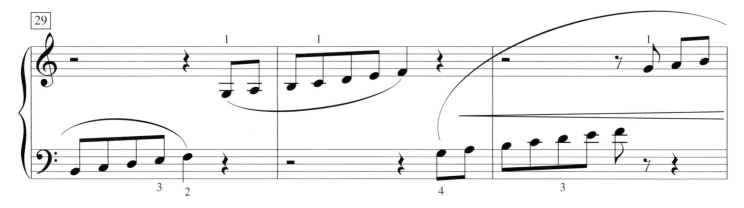

Jin - gle, jin - gle, jin - gle, you will

hear my sleigh bells ring, I am old Kris

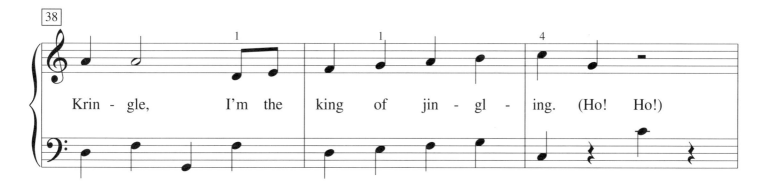

Krin - gle, I'm the king of jin - gl - ing. (Ho! Ho!)

King of jin - gl - ing.

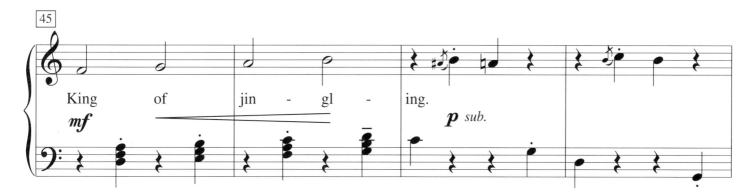

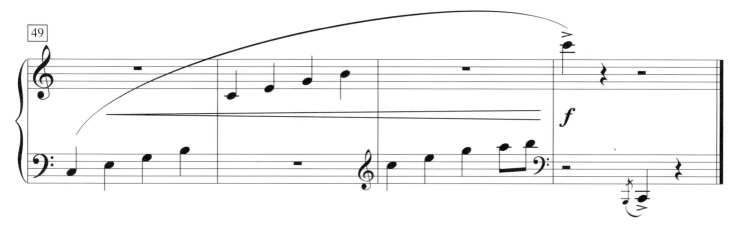

Christmas Is

Use after page 65.

Lyrics by Spence Maxwell
Music by Percy Faith
Arranged by Glenda Austin

Flowing and smooth

poco rit.

Christ-mas is sleigh-bells,

f a tempo

Christ-mas is shar-ing,

Christ-mas is hol - ly,

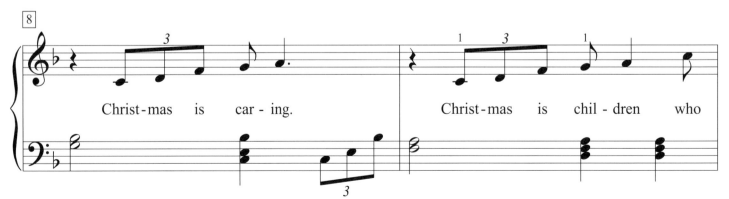

Christ-mas is car - ing.

Christ-mas is chil - dren who

just can't ___ go to sleep; Christ - mas is mem - 'ries, the

kind you ___ al - ways keep. Deck the halls and ___ give a

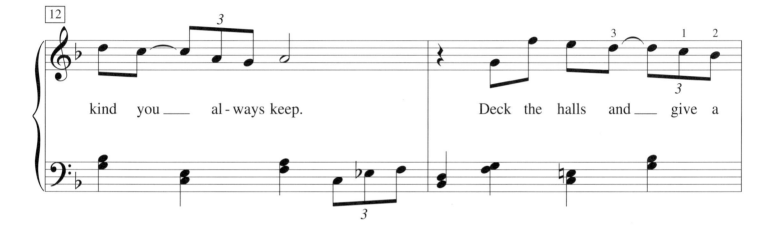

cheer for all the things that Christ-mas is each year.

Christ - mas, ___ Mer - ry Christ - mas, ___ when

mp

Christ-mas, _ Merry Christ-mas, _ when all your wish-es come

true. Christ-mas, __ Mer-ry Christ-mas, _ may

all your wish-es come true.

Because It's Christmas
(For All the Children)
Use after page 75.

Music by Barry Manilow
Lyric by Bruce Sussman and Jack Feldman
Arranged by Glenda Austin

Flowing

To - night the stars shine for the chil - dren, ____
To - night be - longs to all the chil - dren. ____

and light the way for dreams to fly.
To - night their joy runs through the air.

To-night our love comes wrapped in rib -
And so we send our ten - der bless -

- bons. ____
- ings ____

The world is right and hopes are high.
to all the chil - dren ev -'ry - where.

And from a dark _ and frost-ed | win - dow   a child _ ap- | pears   to search _ the
To   see the smiles _ and hear the | laugh - ter,   a time _ to | give,   a time _ to

sky   be - cause _ it's | Christ - mas,   be - cause it's | Christ - mas.
share,   be - cause _ it's   *poco rit.*

2.

Christ - mas   for now _ and for- | ev - er   for all _ of the | chil - dren   and for the

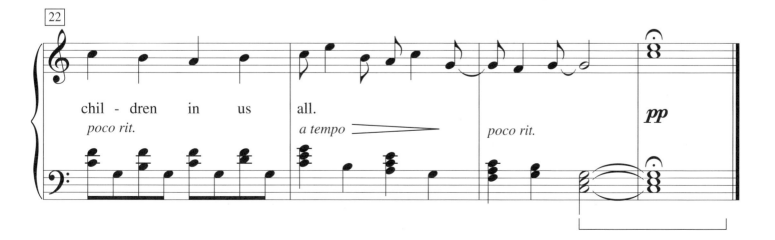

chil - dren   in us   all. | |
poco rit.   *a tempo*   *poco rit.*   *pp*

CLASSICAL PIANO SOLOS

Original Keyboard Pieces from Baroque to the 20th Century

Compiled and edited by Philip Low, Sonya Schumann, and Charmaine Siagian

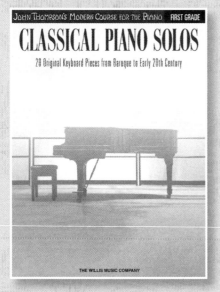

First Grade

22 pieces: *Bartók*: A Conversation • *Mélanie Bonis*: Miaou! Ronron! • *Burgmüller*: Arabesque • *Handel*: Passepied • *d'Indy*: Two-Finger Partita • *Köhler*: Andantino • *Müller*: Lyric Etude • *Ryba*: Little Invention • *Schytte*: Choral Etude; Springtime • *Türk*: I Feel So Sick and Faint, and more!
00119738 / $6.99

Second Grade

22 pieces: *Bartók*: The Dancing Pig Farmer • *Beethoven*: Ecossaise • *Bonis*: Madrigal • *Burgmüller*: Progress • *Gurlitt*: Etude in C • *Haydn*: Dance in G • *d'Indy*: Three-Finger Partita • *Kirnberger*: Lullaby in F • *Mozart*: Minuet in C • *Petzold*: Minuet in G • *Purcell*: Air in D Minor • *Rebikov*: Limping Witch Lurking • *Schumann*: Little Piece • *Schytte*: A Broken Heart, and more!
00119739 / $6.99

Third Grade

20 pieces: *CPE Bach*: Presto in C Minor • *Bach/Siloti*: Prelude in G • *Burgmüller*: Ballade • *Cécile Chaminade*: Pièce Romantique • *Dandrieu*: The Fifers • *Gurlitt*: Scherzo in D Minor • *Hook*: Rondo in F • *Krieger*: Fantasia in C • *Kullak*: Once Upon a Time • *MacDowell*: Alla Tarantella • *Mozart*: Rondino in D • *Rebikov*: Playing Soldiers • *Scarlatti*: Sonata in G • *Schubert*: Waltz in F Minor, and more!
00119740 / $7.99

Fourth Grade

18 pieces: *CPE Bach*: Scherzo in G • *Teresa Carreño*: Berceuse • *Chopin*: Prelude in E Minor • *Gade*: Little Girls' Dance • *Granados*: Valse Poetic No. 6 • *Grieg*: Arietta • *Handel*: Prelude in G • *Heller*: Sailor's Song • *Kuhlau*: Sonatina in C • *Kullak*: Ghost in the Fireplace • *Moszkowski*: Tarentelle • *Mozart*: Allegro in G Minor • *Rebikov*: Music Lesson • *Satie*: Gymnopedie No. 1 • *Scarlatti*: Sonata in G • *Telemann*: Fantasie in C, and more!
00119741 / $7.99

Fifth Grade

19 pieces: *Bach*: Prelude in C-sharp Major • *Beethoven:* Moonlight sonata • *Chopin*: Waltz in A-flat • *Cimarosa*: Sonata in E-flat • *Coleridge-Taylor*: They Will Not Lend Me a Child • *Debussy*: Doctor Gradus • *Grieg*: Troldtog • *Griffes*: Lake at Evening • *Lyadov*: Prelude in B Minor • *Mozart*: Fantasie in D Minor • *Rachmaninoff*: Prelude in C-sharp Minor • *Rameau*: Les niais de Sologne • *Schumann:* Farewell • *Scriabin*: Prelude in D, and more!
00119742 / $8.99

The *Classical Piano Solos* series offers carefully-leveled, original piano works from Baroque to the early 20th century, featuring the simplest classics in Grade 1 to concert-hall repertoire in Grade 5. An assortment of pieces are featured, including familiar masterpieces by Bach, Beethoven, Mozart, Grieg, Schumann, and Bartók, as well as several lesser-known works by composers such as Melanie Bonis, Anatoly Lyadov, Enrique Granados, Vincent d'Indy, Theodor Kullak, and Samuel Coleridge-Taylor.

- Grades 1-4 are presented in a suggested order of study. Grade 5 is laid out chronologically.

- Features clean, easy-to-read engravings with clear but minimal editorial markings.

- View complete repertoire lists of each book along with sample music pages at **www.willispianomusic.com**.

The series was compiled to loosely correlate with the *John Thompson Modern Course*, but can be used with any method or teaching situation.

WILLIS MUSIC

EXCLUSIVELY DISTRIBUTED BY
HAL•LEONARD®

Willis Piano Music

Willis Piano

Willis Piano